This book belongs to

_____

Listening Ninja

By Mary Nhin

Pictures by
Jelena Stupar

Some say I'm a great listener. How do you become a great listener, you ask?

Well sometimes, you have to start by being a poor listener. That's what happened to me...

When someone was telling me something important, I wouldn't be able to recall what had just been said.

When someone was talking, I'd interrupt and say what I was thinking. This didn't allow the other person to finish their thought or sentence.

My listening skills only began to improve after a particular incident.

Well... cleaning my ears helped, too!

It was a fine Saturday afternoon when Communication Ninja came by. The plan was to bake a cake.

While Communication Ninja whipped up the sugar and butter, I was talking about my cooking skills.

A Listening E.A.R. stands for:

More Listening than talking

Eye contact

Ask questions

Repeat back what you heard

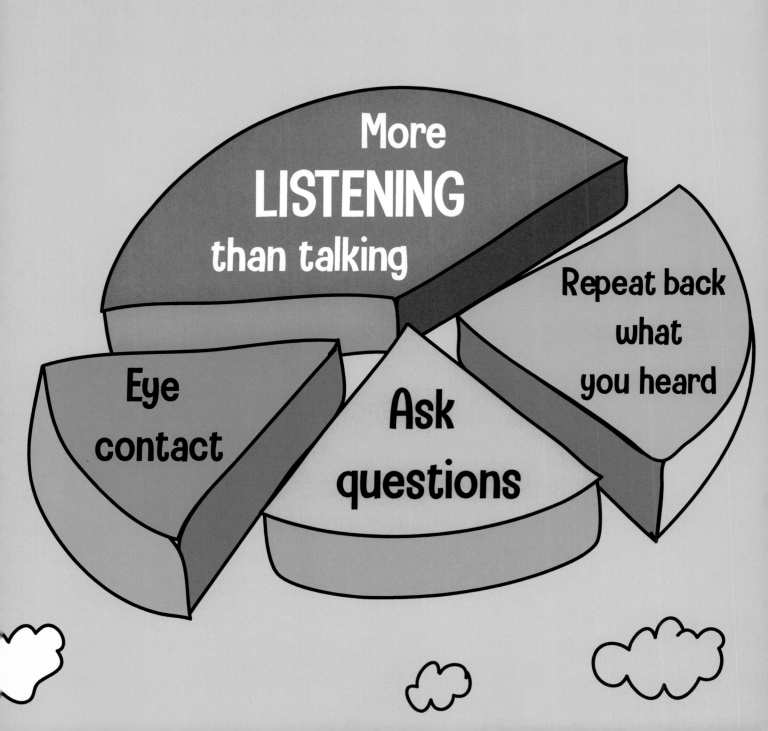

Listening

When we listen more than we talk, we can learn. The more we learn, the better we can serve the other person. If we listen twice as much as we talk, or use a talk/listen ratio of 2:1, we are the ones gaining.

Eye Contact

When we make eye contact with the other person, we show respect and pay attention better.

Asking occasional questions helps us to understand what the other person is saying.

Repeat back what you heard
It's good to repeat what the other person has said just to make sure you heard them correctly.

The next day my mom was telling me a story about my grandpa. I focused my eyes on my mom and made a decision to listen more than I talked.

My mom continued the story while I asked a couple of questions and repeated back what I heard.

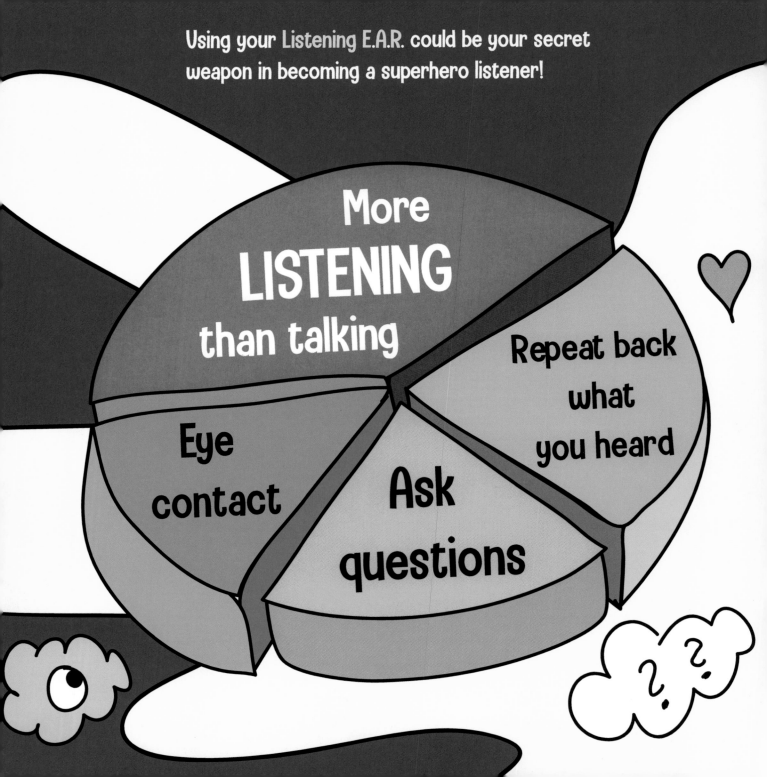

Please visit us at ninjalifehacks.tv
to check out our box sets!

@marynhin   @GrowGrit
#NinjaLifeHacks

Mary Nhin   Ninja Life Hacks

Ninja Life Hacks

Printed in Great Britain
by Amazon

70542049R00020